SONIA O'SULLIVAN

running to
stand still

storytime

Here is a sports story but it's a love story too.

If you've ever watched Sonia O' Sullivan, watched her once on a good day you've seen some of the love. Of running and of racing. It's written on her face and in her flashing eyes and fluid stride. When she goes, when she kicks , it's a wild feral thing and it's beautiful to watch. People lean forward in their seats and clench their fists. There are few greater sights in sport than watching Sonia do what she loves to do.

One late summers day recently she won a silver medal at the Olympics.

It was one of those occasions. Nation as village. Children were herded into assembly halls to watch. Office workers gathered around small televisions. College students gathered on concourses. Traffic stopped.

The woman in whom Ireland had invested so much emotion and hope was on the track again. People roared and people cried. Adults watched from behind the cracks in their own fingers. People turned away from the screen. Too raw.

Go on girl!

Silver. "So close", said Sonia, and then broke into a smile that spread across the face of the country that loves her.

Silver. Bronze. Last. Didn't matter. She'd just run faster than we thought possible. She'd just laid herself bare again. She was back.

Ireland's greatest ever athlete, restored.

Sports story. Love story.

"It wouldn't have mattered if Sonia had come last" said her partner Nick Bideau with their daughter Ciara playful in his arms "Because we're happy."

This is the story of recovered happiness. The story of a kid from Cobh who grew up deeply in love with the business of running and racing. She grew to be the best runner in the world, indomitable, brave, imperious.

World champion. Olympic favourite. Then she had her heart and spirit broken.

When Sonia O' Sullivan cracked that smile on the finish line in Sydney it was the end of a journey marked by so many tears.

Atlanta. Athens. Turin. Many points between. All those places we followed her to as she fell apart and tried to put herself back together again and again. Slowly. Piece by piece. When she crossed the line in Sydney she finished her redemption song, pronounced herself free, free at last.

If you'd written her obituary in 1996, you would have noted that she was too great and too pure an athlete to have had a prime of just two seasons but too obsessed and too consumed a figure to make herself last longer.

"I can't accept that there are things I cannot do," she said once before she self-destructed "I just think that if I work harder I can do anything."

Re-assembling herself meant being easier on herself, less obsessive.

Getting better meant sharing her life, not shutting it off.

When she crossed the finish line in Sydney she wrote the last words of the best Irish sports story that we've known. Well, much more than a mere sports story from more than a mere athlete. A love story.

19.03.2000 alone at the end of the 4km race, world cross country championships, vilamoura, portugal

this girl's life

They'd meet every evening at the wall on the corner of Wilmount Park, a big harum-scarum posse of Cobh kids. There was Sonia O'Sullivan, Deirdre O'Mahony, Lisa O'Donovan, Christine Butler and so on. Growing up with long dreamy amber evenings to put down.

Kids. They played eternal games of hide and seek. The lawns of Wilmount Park stretched out in a long tempting ribbon behind them. They'd hide in gardens 'till somebody was spotted and then whoosh! Off from the coverts like a Grand National field, sprites hurdling down the street, leaping over bushes and fences. Hurdling and whooping.

Those fun splashed summer evenings are the first thing she remembers about the feeling of running, the sheer, flat-out, headlong rushing thrill of it. It gripped her then and never let go.

They got older and more mischievous. Knocking on peoples' doors and hiding before they could answer. The old hilarity. People noticed that Sonia O'Sullivan had the pace of a colt so any house with a long front garden was her responsibility. Run Sonia, run.

Races. It started with the Community Games, a nun and a big box of lollipops. That was the prize, a chance to dip a hand into a box and pull out a lollipop. Sonia O'Sullivan was an 'also-ran' but everyone got a lollipop. Sister Rosario walked through the clamour with her box of

14.08.2000 barrack hill, cobh, county cork, ireland

imps under her oxter and they swarmed around her with slender arms reaching. Sister! Sister! Sister!

It finishes here maybe, here in this coliseum for a new Millennium. Slightly crouched at a starting line under the charcoal tarp of an Australian sky. Homebush Bay, Sydney. Sonia O'Sullivan's face being pumped into television sets in every corner of the world. That face tells her story. She's wired for what's ahead, honed by what lies behind.

The Olympics! Too big to imagine. She nestles her own thoughts. This race, this collection of straights and bends and a finish line, this is the stage which will define a life, a running life which has been marked by many sweet victories and a handful of immense defeats. It needs an exclamation mark at the end!

Cobh. Annually, for charity, they used run around the island, a ten mile round trip on a Sunday afternoon. It was called the Milk Run because when you'd get to the back of the island they'd have brimming churns of milk set out there and every athlete would down a big glass of milk ladled straight out. With distended guts they'd take half a day to finish after that.

Once upon a Milk Run, long ago now, Sonia O'Sullivan was loping along on her own when a gentleman stranger looked her up and down before passing her.

"You know," he said, "you'd probably be pretty good at cross-country running."

"And what's that?" she said, thinking that he was proposing that she run across the entire country.

He told her. She laughed. The sliver was in her bloodstream though. At 13 she ran a cross-country race in faraway Midleton, fell in love with the feel of footfall on grass.

Addicted. Waylaid by flu she'd stifle her shivering and spluttering long enough to convince her mother that she could go into the fields and run. She'd finish and wheeze doubled over outside the house for half an hour before swinging through the door whistling. Never better Ma, never better. She ran in cowfields. Always in barefeet. The feeling never leaves, the feeling of being covered in scabs of cowdung, the sensation of cowdung squeezing up between the toes. They don't show that in the Nike ads. She'd bring a towel but come home looking like the wall of a cow shed anyway. First pair of spikes. Unspeakable glamour. Her father had tried to put his football boots in the washing machine once so it was off limits. Every time the spikes went into the sink to be washed tenderly. She never thought of that until before the second cross-country race in Marrakech in 1998 when she found herself washing spikes and daydreaming. Something about the ritual of it, made her think of all those cross-country races for Ballymore-Cobh as a young girl, all those evenings running the hills with homework rattling in her head. Theorems. Poems. French grammar. Everything subjugated to running. Running. What she does and what she is and what has brought her here to an Olympic starting line. Just now that patch of track on the floor of the stadium is maybe the loneliest place in the world. Coaches, friends, training partners, family, fans, there is nothing they can do now. Every runner unravels the race that's ahead for her knowing that failure never has a bigger audience.

In the beginning, ah, everything was local. She had her picture in the local paper when she was fourteen. The Munster schools cross-country in Dungarvan. She'd won and there next week was her picture. A little shot of glamour. She remembers the blow of discovering that there was to be no All-Ireland series for Under 14's. If you won Munster and had your picture in the paper, you'd surely win the All-Ireland.

It was always local stuff. The Olympics didn't exist. "When I was 13, I was on a cross-country team competing against England, Scotland and Wales. We won. Beating England was always as big as we could imagine. We stayed in a hotel in Kent and after the race we had a water balloon fight among ourselves. Nobody had been away from home by themselves before and nobody knew if they would be again. We never thought about careers. None of us did. Even later, in America doing an athletics scholarship in Villanova, I imagined I would be an accountant. I came home once after three years and my mother made me write to every accountancy firm in Cork looking for a summer job. That seemed reasonable."

Now they lean forward a little bit more. She can feel shoulders rubbing against hers anticipating the jostle ahead. All their lives have led to this moment. A world watching and you can hear your own heartbeat. The stadium so quiet in anticipation. She listens and waits, listens and waits. Tells herself one last time what she has to do. She balls her hands into fists and waits for that old prompt, that familiar signal. Bang!

14.08.2000 bird's hill, cobh, county cork, ireland

leaving home

Things you never forget: First day at school, first boyfriend, first kiss, first coach.

Pat O'Halloran was a gangly long jumper and maybe ten years older than the kids he trained. He'd take them to the track or to a race and always it was an outing. On the way home they'd stop in Mandy's on the corner of Patrick Street in Cork, and being healthy athletes they'd have fishburgers with their chips, the diet of champions.

He took them to roller-discos. Pat would disco dance while they flew around bumping into each other and laughing. Fishburgers and roller-discos were key activities. And the club end of year party. And trips to Youghal, driving past the funfair on the way home, whining in chorus to be allowed stop. They had good teams back then, they won trophies everywhere for cross-country and relays but never cared too much about winning. They'd finish second sometimes if they thought that the runners-up trophy looked nicer.

For treats there were the International meets in Fermoy. Starring Miruts "The Shifter" Yifter. The girls from Cobh ogled the fellas running around. The trophies would be laid out on groaning tables like a crowded cemetery and they'd stand there for the longest while, picking out the nice ones. Highlight of the evening.

Sonia grew quick and serious. She heard stories about Sean Kennedy making people run up hills at the back of the reservoir. Hard man. That sounded good. She called him up.

He'd write out two weeks worth of training, photocopy it and if she didn't see him he'd slip the instructions in the letterbox on his way to work. Sean worked all hours down in Cara Partners in Little Island. Sonia never knew what it was they did there but she won a seven mile road race once which Cara had sponsored. Won a slide projector. What's a kid to do with a slide projector? She sold it for £100.

27.01.2000 langford's gap, falls creek, australia

27.01.2000 garage, falls creek, australia

Sean Kennedy devoured books by Peter Coe, digesting every lesson that Sebastian Coe digested. Sonia received it all as gospel. She has an old training log at home earnestly filled with unlikely stats. "200 metres in 28 seconds", "300 metres in 36 seconds." Impossible stuff for a kid. She'd picture what 100 metres might be like on the grass field and then add on a bit in her head for longer distances and swoosh! Look out world!

She was a special talent though, the dominant runner of her generation in Ireland. They'd talk for hours plotting what races she should run, what sessions she should be doing, where she should be heading. Sean Kennedy and Sonia O'Sullivan, sitting in the car, sitting at a kitchen table, walking the fields, planning the next step.

Finally schooldays finished. College beckoned. Villanova, a cradle of Irish middle distance running crooked its finger.

Leaving home and all that. Sean Kennedy spoke to Sonia and told her that from then on Marty Stern would be her coach. Fine. She arrived in America on crutches suffering from a hairline fracture and after two years of Marty Stern and hard running on tracks her legs were getting more fragile. The phone calls to Sean Kennedy grew more frequent.

He suggested running on the grass. He suggested "fartleks", the oddly named system of short improvised unstructured training bursts. Jazz for athletes. Fartleks. Ar nos na gaoithe.

Sonia was chafing. She yearned for the heavy sessions. 5 X1000 metres as an appetiser. Gutbusters. Marty Stern would listen to the proposals and acidly observe that he wouldn't give a workout like that to a horse.

So under cover of Sean Kennedy's curative Fartleks she would disappear off onto the grass and basically do as she wished. She ran the Big East conference, qualified for regionals and went to the US Nationals and finished third. "These Fartleks are a wonder," pronounced Marty. In 1991 she was World Student Games Champion. A pure wonder.

Villanova disappeared in the rear-view mirror. Sean Kennedy trained Sonia for the Barcelona

Olympics in 1992. That memorable Olympic final night. Sonia O'Sullivan from Cobh bounding away like a deer on a prairie only to be roped in by cannier runners. Fourth place but a famous face now.

Her innocent audacity in Barcelona earned her a spot on the great merry-go-round. After Barcelona she ran everywhere. Non-stop racing just going from one track to another running on adrenaline and excitement.

She had met Kim McDonald in Lille in France after a mile race in 1991. Kim was representing Marcus O'Sullivan and Frank O'Mara so they knew each other by reputation. Sonia ran a poor race, in Lille hanging onto the back and having to pass a whole load of people on the last lap. Kim was keen to point out straight away what a negative race it was. Cheeky hoor, she thought.

Late 1992. The music stopped and she went back to work. Sean Kennedy faxed programmes to London. The world had changed though. She was training with other athletes, sniffing out their routines, borrowing stuff. Through 1993 she found herself asking Kim McDonald questions about this or that. McDonald's solid career and his stable of successful Kenyans gave him the aura of guru. She went to the track one day and was undecided about doing 5 x 800 or a series stepping down from 1000 metres to 600 metres, followed by 400 metres twice. She wrote a note to Kim and asked which she should do. He said do this. And do it in these times.

"I started training with Kenyan girls and became involved with a different group. I drifted from Sean. I never discussed it with him or talked about it which I suppose I should have done. I ran in the Cork City Sports and lost to Aisling Molloy. I talked to Sean after that. I was really annoyed. He told me that one bad race didn't make me a bad runner. I said to him that obviously I had a different coach now. I needed to do different things. It's one of the hardest things to do like breaking up with a boyfriend. You don't want to hurt their feelings or not be their friend but you're telling them that somebody else is better for you. I think Sean knew. We never had a problem but I worried that there might be a problem."

23.04.2000 balmoral, scotland

falls creek

1998 in Falls Creek. Another New Year filled with fresh resolution. Out running one day Steve Moneghetti unspooled his philosophy of things to Sonia. Running was not about thinking of the result but thinking about, how, right now you could run the best possible race, how you could get deep under the skin of the race and into the music of running. "Stop thinking about winning." he said, "Think about how you'll get to that finish line. If you are good enough, your way will get you there first but you don't need to know that before you run."

She used to need to know that, used to have to run fast in training all the time, just to know that. Train hard, win easy, the Kenyans would say. Nobody trained harder. Most of the time she won easy.

Falls Creek is a place of renewal. In the middle of the Australian alps, 350 kilometres north east of Melbourne, up the Hume Highway 'till you turn off at Snow Road. The piste rats clear off the powdery slopes for the Australian summer and the stringy distance freaks arrive, stopping at the last available supermarket, stocking up provisions to last a while.

Falls Creek is hardcore Australia. The names announce the feel. Wombats Ramble. Bogong High Plains Road. Snowgums Lane. The countryside is scattered with lodges filled up by the running community. Most of them arrive up the day after Christmas. Can't wait to be 5,000 feet above sea level, sucking that skinny air.

There's a first day feel that everyone has experienced. Filled with determination you might hit the hills and let the macho in you take over. You'll be rewarded with pains in your head, nausea, dizziness. The whole gift range delivered express from Altitude.com. Happy New Year.

The wise ones find their own rhythms. Monday, Wednesday and Friday, Sonia and company drive the five minutes haul to Langfords Gap where the good running trails follow the aqueducts that supply the area with water.

You can run east or west; it depends on the day. You meet fine, big cows, bred huge on all the good air. No kangaroos or koalas, just giant cows! At the end of the run the athletes go into the damned area of the aqueduct and stand in the ice cold water with running shorts clinging to goose-pimpled skin. The freezing blackness laps gently about them getting the blood pumping to tired muscles. It's so cold it must be doing some good, they tell each other.

In the evenings they leave again at 5.30 for a half-hour run from the little village along different aqueduct trails. Just a recovery run. Then exercises and dinner. The high life.

It's a place of purging, as much spiritual as athletic. In 1998 she went there and Steve Moneghetti's words lodged in her head. For the first time she could accommodate them in her vision of running. She saw the compatibility of Moneghetti's philosophy with what Alan Storey had been urging her to do and decided then that Alan Storey's words would shape the rest of her career.

No more leaving her soul spread thin over the training track.

27.01.2000 langford's gap, falls creek, australia

the machine

"Sonia, you're skinny out."

"You're like a twig girl."

Skinny out and tall too. Schooldays emphasised the gawkiness in everyone and everyone emphasised the gawkiness in each other. "Sonia you haven't a pick on ya girl."

Her teens marked the war of yearnings. Wanting to be smaller and curvier yet wanting to be faster.

Discos. She'd feel like a big weedy giant with her head bopping up above the crowd, her elbows in people's faces.

Her body made most sense to her when she was running. Athlete's limbs, athlete's bones, athlete's metabolism. The usual allocation of limbs and the usual arrangement of bones. Why worry? The leg bone's connected to the kneebone, the kneebone's connected to the thighbone, the thighbone's connected to the hipbone and so on. Yet it was an athlete's set. Lean and ready to be sharpened.

Her body. These days it weighs about 55 kgs in summer and more if you catch her in winter. That's her official estimate anyway. She seldom climbs on a scales during the season. Too easy to get hung up. Don't tinker with the machine if you don't have to.

Lots of women runners have gone down that road. It's temptingly easy. "In Florida once I went half a week just eating three apples a day. As a runner you find you can eat very little for a few days and lose a pile of weight quickly. You don't think further than that sometimes."

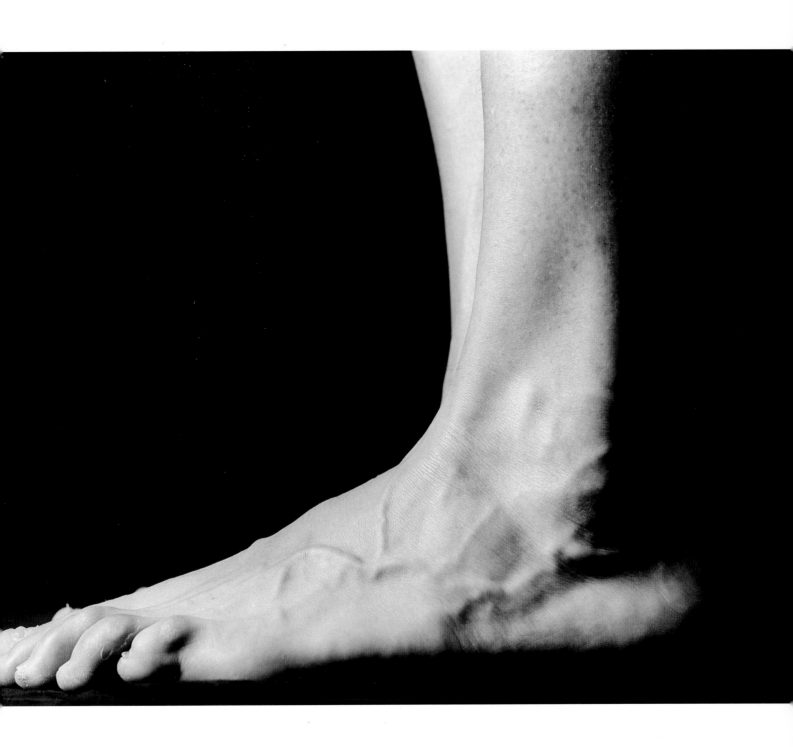

She never flirted with serious diet problems but her intake was never the result of the appliance of science either. She used think that if she went as long as possible without eating anything after a training session and then stocked up on proteins and carbohydrates she'd done herself a favour. Other times she'd decide to manage on fruit and veg for as long as she could. Now she just listens to what her body says.

Mostly.

Not long ago she went for an X-ray on a sore foot. At the best of times you can look at an athlete's foot and you get an idea of its owner's career. At the specialists though they were dumbstruck. The pictures came back and Sonia could see them gathering around to gawp.

"Oh you've broken your foot before," he said when he finally got her sitting down.

"No I haven't."

"Oh I'm afraid you have. Lots of times."

And he showed her the picture. Horror show. A conglomeration of bumps and lines all over the left foot. She just sat there gaping.

What kind of foot is this?

A foot full of broken bones.

Five stress fractures in the left foot he reckoned. That's every bone in each leg, up and down and back again she's broken. Shins, tibias, femurs. The lot. The left foot completed the collection.

And she'd thought it was just her right foot had that kind of topography. She has

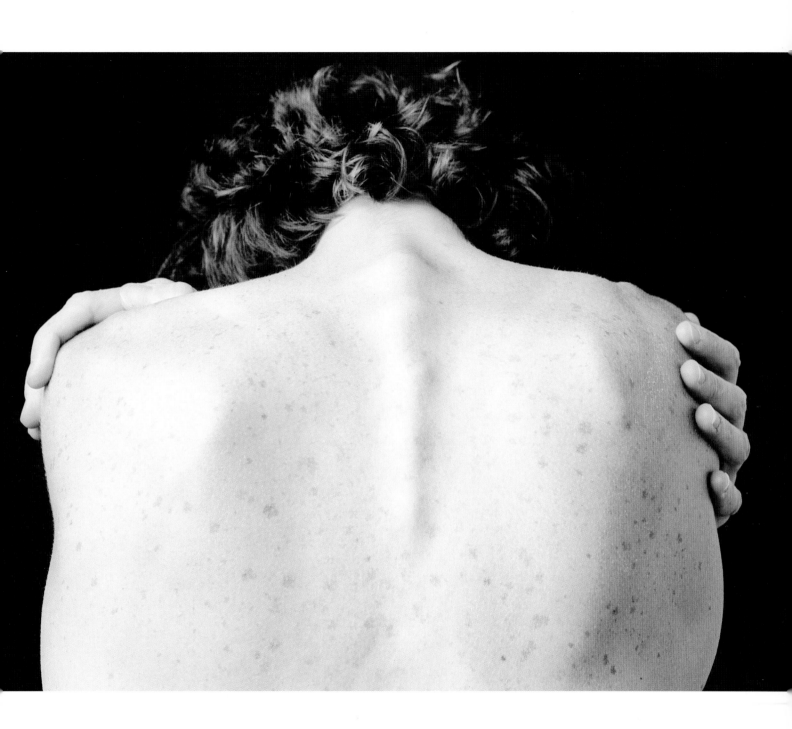

a massive lump on her right foot that screams in pain if she wears normal shoes. It's the legacy of a college stress fracture which she just kept running on until a massive calcium deposit grew up. Nike have made these spikes that are like stockings, they fit over the foot and stretch so there's nothing pushing. She wears them for racing.

The bump and grind of the running life. She remembers the bad injuries only starting with the first one, a broken shin back in 1987, a week before the European Junior Championships in Birmingham. A back injury in late 1999. An Achilles tendon injury in late 1995 and early 1996. Sometimes a pain means nothing, it flees after a good session, sometimes it costs six weeks and for a runner that's half a lifetime.

Olympic year demands caution. All year she's been having blood tests partly as a favour to Brian Moore, a medical student from Galway who's doing experiments in St Mary's College in Twickenham. He's been testing athletes studying their blood and monitoring them. Sonia goes every four weeks. He does a census on her haemoglobin and iron levels and whatever else.

Everything has been good. She eats more red meat occasionally making up a stew with some beef and some liver in it hoping to smuggle the liver past the taste buds without them noticing.

"I'm thirty now and I know I've pushed my body too hard at times. Sometimes it's been crying out and I've ignored it. Late in the 1994 season I was running on empty. I know when the batteries have gone because I get cold sores on my lip. I wanted to keep going though, to wring the best out of the year so I went to Paris for the Grand Prix final. I remember hurting so badly. Catherina McKiernan caught me. I gritted my teeth and just hung on. I finished but I felt as bad as I've ever felt and have often wondered if pushing so hard in 1994 laid the seeds for what would happen in 1996. A few more years is all my body needs to give me, then I'll give it back its body fat and its rest and its right to refuse liver"

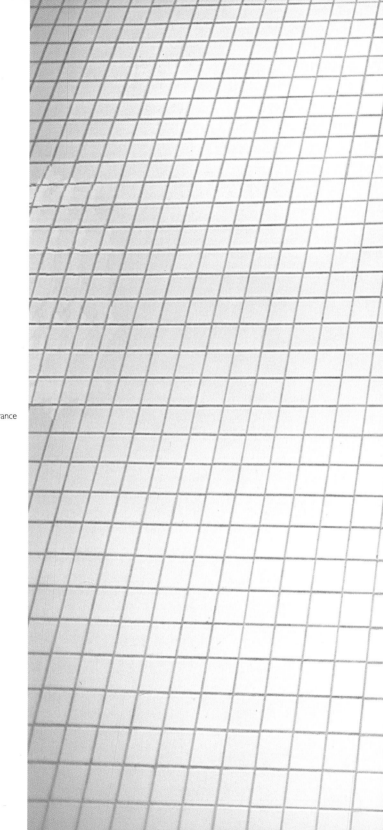

23.06.2000 hotel forest la villette, paris, france

24.06.2000 end of training run, parc de la villette, paris, france

19.07.2000 in gym at home, east molsley, surrey, england

a day at the office

PART I.

Norway. Oslo. Bislett Games. 1500 metres. 9pm

A timetable. She works backwards. Evening to morning. Race at nine. Race after dark. So train at eleven. Yeah. Dawdle over breakfast. Train at eleven. This will be a long day's journey into pain. This will be a key day.

Oslo. It's been a while but, hey, same old, same old. Same hotel. Same faces. Same track. Same crazy crowds. She scopes her hotel room. Empties her kit bag and lays everything on a chair.

Spikes. This week it rained spikes. Nike mailed her a pair and she trained in them on Tuesday. Almost perfect. She e-mailed Nike for the correct size. Spikes arrived all week, three pairs waiting in the hotel, slender sheaths that leave no weight on your foot.

Singlet and shorts. No number yet, just a swoosh and a brand name. Her epitaph will have a footnote concerning singlets and shorts and the fact of her federation once forcing her to strip out of one pair in an Olympic stadium in Atlanta. Years on she laughs when she thinks of it. In Sydney she'll wear "something green."

Waterbottle. Tracksuit top. Spare clothes. The things she carries. They wait on a chair for their moment.

Raceday breakfast equals coffee and cereal. Coffee is good. Cereal is necessary. She lingers. She changes. She rides the elevator.

Lobby. John Mayock and Hayley Tullett are stretching for their morning runs. She joins them. Living sculptures in the foyer. They run for twenty minutes and when they come back she goes out to meet Robert Kibet and William Tanui. Runs back with them. Why run more? Because she does, because she always does.

Showers. Changes. Goes to bed with Harry Potter. Eats lunch at 2.30. Two tomato and cheese sandwiches. Crackers. Jam. Tea. Back to bed with Harry. Wearing spikes this time, to break them in. Coffee at five. Tick. Tick. Tick.

6:55 p.m. Racing uniform says goodbye to chair.

7:00pm Sonia says hello to shuttle bus.

7:15pm Sonia dropped off at gate to Bislett Stadium.

This crazy bandbox of a stadium. She's lit it up more than once. Sitting on stone steps she watches other races until the cold seeps into her thighs. She wanders into the little room for athletes, lies down and reads Athletics Weekly with her legs up against the wall. Tick. Tick. Tick.

8:05pm Stretches the limbs. Catlike. Outside the girls are running on the triangle of gravel in the corner. Looks like half a prison yard. Hectic dodgems. She leaves the stadium and walks to the park that she knows must still be there. Runs two serene laps.

8:43pm Checks in. Oslo is still easy-going. No holding rooms. No blazers handcuffed heroically to athletes. She walks onto the track. Keeps moving. Keeps thinking. Trina Hattestad of Norway throws the javelin further than any woman ever has before. A tsunami of hysteria rolls around the Bislett. She keeps thinking. Keeps thinking.

8:55pm Strides up and down the back straight. No time left. Big strides. Kids in tracksuits bring the athletes' gear and waterbottles away in baskets. This flock of stringy women move towards the start line. No escape now.

Nobody says anything. Even good friends have only the space to insert oneliners into the tension. She talks to herself. Over and over.

The mantra of what she is going to do: Run fast and strong.

The mantra of what she is not going to do: Be nervous or get boxed in.

Relax. Relax. Relax. Keep making left turns and you'll get there. At the line Suzy Favor-Hamilton says: "I saw your baby. Oh she's absolutely gorgeous."

Nice funny woman.

9:00pm The crack of the pistol. The start is chaos. Rubber scorching off the track for 100 metres. Shock to the system. What it does is, it hurts. She had told herself it was going to hurt. Really hurt. Ignore it, ignore it, she says now. Keep going. It bloody hurts.

Can't get to the front early. Not great. Stay cool girl, stay cool. In the second lap the Polish girl moves up. Follow her. Get bumped out to lane three for going around the top bend. So what?

23.06.2000 hotel forest la villette, paris, france

Lane three is cool. On the inside lanes she's not happy. It kills her. The gun goes and everyone jostles for the inside. You can go straight up and and cut in later but nobody has the guts. They cut to the inside like it's the last exit in an inferno. Lane three. Fine. She has a manager who knows she likes the outside. He lets them know. She usually gets the outside. She wonders about the wisdom. In the Olympics you take what you get. Should she practice bumping and grinding and spiking? Not now.

Two laps. Feeling good. Big posse in front. Everyone fancying it now. The feet make a nice pitter-patter percussion on the tartan. Good pace she thinks. Her body knows the routine now.

She holds on but there is a heartbeat, no more, when concentration flees. Leaves no note. Just a gap.

Last lap. She's chasing. Chasing doesn't feel as good as overtaking. No surge. Her gut is bursting. The finish is crazy. Down the straight. Noise everywhere. She's catching them but she runs out of track and crosses into the world of post mortems in ninth place.

Learns that her time is 4:01.7. Heart sings. "Oslo made me happy. All the laps were practically the same time. I felt good at the end. The strength training gave me something. I could have kept going like that for a while, pounding them out. Ninth place? I'm not a 1500-metre runner today. I have my own agenda. I've met it."

PART II

Eight days later. London on a Saturday afternoon.

Is there any hint of calamity in the air? Not really. On Thursday she felt bad in training but sometimes you just feel bad. Two days before your last 5000 metre race in your Olympic preparations, you grit your teeth and take the pain. She'd worked hard at the track on Tuesday. Just how hard would remain a source of tension between Nick Bideau and Alan Storey for months. Anyway by Thursday she knows her legs were sulking.

Maybe it's just nerves she says. She goes to bed and hordes her energy.

Friday. She travels to the meet hotel. Feeling good, well better.

It's Saturday, she's trackside and the breeze is in her face. This is a race brimming with big names. TV cameras and journalists have been attracted like filings to a magnet.

The place hums with rumours. Cathy Freeman has pulled out of the 400 metres.

So has Katherine Merry.

The adrenaline bubbles up inside. This will be a day to send a message.

The first few laps she feels good. She samples the pace and she can master it. She can bend this race to her will. Knew this was going to be a good day, knew it.

08.07.2000 start line, 3000m, nikaia 2000 grand prix, nice, france

Then the weakness waylays her. Stomach pains and weary legs and uncertainty.

Déjà vu. Faint reminders of bad times gone by.

"I don't want this to happen," she says to herself.

She trails home in ninth. A ninth place bereft of any warm consolation. She finishes in a time she'll never look at again without feeling disgust.

She tells the world she's not been well this past few days, that she'll be back. Yet notebooks and satellites are already filled with the words of her obituary. Her final 5000 metres of the summer has swilled off down the drain.

She shrugs for the cameras. She can't sleep, can't work this one out. She sees the uselessness of things which can't be undone. She sees the end of it all.

However hard she'd trained it doesn't yield up the same confidence that winning a good race does. She'd needed that.

Duly she worried it to death, rifled the air for a positive she could draw from the ruins of Crystal Palace. Zurich, loomed urgent and glamorous the following Wednesday. The big meet of the Grand Prix season, a showcase of form and intention. By Sunday night Sonia was convinced that not only was Zurich a waste of time but the rest of the season was. If she couldn't get past the top eight in a 5000 metre field after all she'd put in, well maybe it wasn't going to happen.

"My immediate reaction was that I shouldn't run. Not in Zurich. Probably not for the rest of the season. I'd run that bad and I didn't want to run that bad again. On the Sunday I went for a run and I came back and I started to think that maybe I should run. I just needed to find out for certain if I was finished."

She spoke with Alan Storey, unburdening a mind teeming with dark thoughts. He advised a rest, even told her the best place to get one. "Go to Kew Forest," he said "and think about things."

Alan's words always weighed heavier than he thought. All summer he had told Sonia the best time she had inside her before a race. All summer he had been right. Now she'd confounded him in the last way she would have wished to. She'd run lousy. Even Alan seemed at a loss. He said he'd call Kim and tell him that Sonia wouldn't be going to Zurich. Sonia went home.

"I thought I have to find out is there something really wrong with me. Do I really want to do this? Can I go in these races and get my head around winning them. Maybe I didn't have that thing when I got to the hard part, maybe I didn't have the guts to keep up."

Once she was a kid who never saw a race she didn't like, a fight she wouldn't take on and now she wondered if she still had guts.

ZURICH

Monday night. Bed but no peace. A thousand and one thoughts marathoning through her head. Stuff she never imagined. Running is sustenance to her.

Stopping, the thought of it, a trauma.

"I knew if I didn't run in Zurich I wouldn't run for the rest of the year. I really thought that was the end. If I had trained so hard and hadn't improved at all it was the end. I couldn't live with it being the end. I felt that I had to run in Zurich to put myself back on the line again, just to see one last time. If I rested and rested and ran hard maybe..."
She jumped out of bed at three in morning.

Sent an e-mail to Alan.
Sent an e-mail to Kim.

"Maybe Alan has talked you. I think I'm going to run in Zurich. Here are the reasons..."

She went back to bed. Cold sheets. No sleep. "Here are the reasons"? The certainty that possessed her at the keyboard was gone again. Her whole career came jangling through her mind. She woke Nick and told him that she had to run in Zurich.

"I won't find out anything without facing it down."

Early next morning she calls Kim McDonald.

"So have you spoken to Alan?"
"No"
"Did you get my email?"
"Well not yet. I haven't checked."
"Well I'm going to Zurich."
"Of course."

She decided to raise the bar a little and chose to call up two journalists and tell them that she was fine and looking forward to Zurich. She lifted the phone:

"Hi. This is Sonia. Listen everything is fine. I'm going to run in Zurich and I'm really looking forward to it."

Two calls. Two Dublin journalists so surprised that they hadn't reams of questions with which to detain her. She found herself speaking on her terms.

She put down the phone and felt the benefit of the exercise immediately. There would be no reversing out of Zurich.

She goes to Zurich early. Rests. Prepares perfectly. Warms up effectively. Runs 8:27 for the 3000. Finishes a close second to Szabo. E-Mails everyone:

`8:27! 2nd, Felt Fantastic.`

"I'd asked Alan before London what he expected of me. He said you can run close to your best. All summer I'd been asking him that and he was right all along. He'd tell me what I had in me and I would run that time. So then to go in London and run so bad. I ran worse than I should have. There was a point where I threw in the towel, I just wanted to disappear and not be there anymore. I was such a quitter right there and I nearly packed it all in. I didn't want to know. I had to learn from there that if you're not going to win the race you have to try to be second and if you can't be second be third."

She'd forgotten about Steve Moneghetti and the wisdom of Falls Creek. She wasn't hearing the music of the races anymore.

"Stop thinking about winning," he'd said. "Think about how you'll get to that finish line. If you are good enough your way will get you there first but you don't need to know that before you run".

After Zurich the rhythms were stirring her blood again.

08.07.2000 after finishing 4th,3000m, nikaia 2000 grand prix, nice, france

sonia inc.

East Germany has evaporated. The Chinese have come and gone. She's still running. Money is everywhere now. Up front and on the table. Track and field is a capitalist state.

Cash.

In the beginning cash was a dirty secret. Runners knew nothing. Cash was like the common cold. You got it or your didn't get it.

Cash.

Some got paid, half guiltily in notes passed under the table or slipped (yes, in brown bags) in with their gear. Got paid or didn't. Whichever. To Sonia O'Sullivan it all seemed like a mystery that didn't involve her and which would probably never involve her.

"When are you going to get a proper job?" her mother used to say.

Whenever. She fended it off but wondered.

Money trickled towards her. She had a year left to do in Villanova and had a little deal going with Reebok. Shoes and gear and if she kept all her receipts then they'd pay her expenses. She came to Ireland for the summer and sent back the receipts. Seemed like a living. Her mother said it was no sort of a life.

Money is complicated. Is now and ever shall be. In America news of her racing in Europe circulated before she could go back to run the final indoor season. Ray Treacy, the coach in Providence called up Marty Stern the coach in Villanova. Ray told Marty that if Sonia O'Sullivan wasn't taken off the indoor team he'd tell the NCAA about her soiled amateurism. She sat out the indoor season. Penance for veniality.

At some point thereafter, she passed under the lintel and into the professional world. She hit the circuit after the Olympics in 1992, just bounced from one track meet to another full as a boot with confidence. She won races. No big money but it was a new sort of life.

Her first proper Grand Prix race was at Crystal Palace in London. Innocent naif. She just fished Andy Norman's number out of a phonebook and called up to ask if she could run in the race. Gave her name and the fact that she'd run 15:26 for a 5K the week before. Waited for him to swoon. Waited long enough to be glad when he just said OK.

She thought that was how things were done until Christy Wall from the BLE called on the phone.

Who gave you permission to talk to Andy Norman?

Well, nobody. Who said I needed permission?

Us.

Her college friend Gina Procaccio was in the race. They spent a week rubbernecking the stars. Half intimidated, half excited. They roomed together, shopped together and chatted together. A couple of tourists doing the Grand prix circuit. If it's Thursday it must be Oslo.

One thing. At Crystal Palace Gina was getting paid $1000 to run in the race. Sonia had worked up the nerve to ask for a couple of tickets for her Auntie. Sonia came fourth and Gina came tenth. Gina got the $1000. Sonia's auntie got the tickets.

Still no way to figure out how this money business worked. She was curious but not curious enough to ask. The secret life of the track.

Cash. She got paid properly for a cross-country in Le Mans, in 1992. The prize was about $2500. She got on a train back to Paris on her own after the race. A girl, a backpack, a cheque and a great big shiny cup. She arrived in Paris with a few hours to kill and wandered around with the cup and the gear looking for a place to have a baguette. If you were a winner in Paris with your first pay-cheque burning holes in your pocket you had to have a baguette. De rigeur.

She hit top form at a good time. Her years of total immersion on the circuit coincided with the unveiling of athletics riches. TV money. Endorsement money. Kit money. Appearance money. It was all out there, sitting in naked wobbly piles on the table. No more high church amateurism or brown bag sinners.

These things a modern athlete does: Runs behind a shopping trolley carrying a camera man on a track in Dallas. Peers for half an hour into a camera lens in Paris trying to look serious. Opens a shop in Dublin making happy chatter with the people. Attaches a dot.com to her name

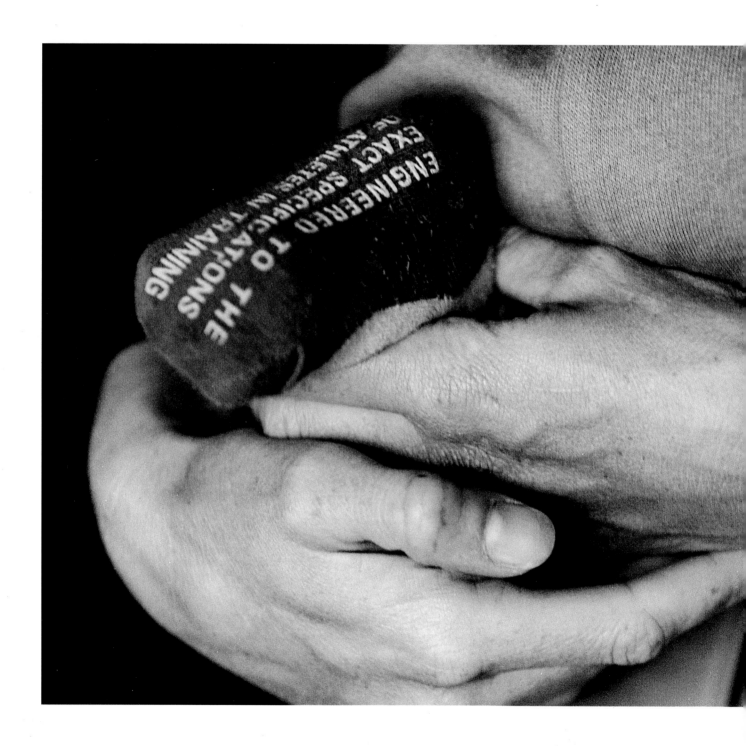

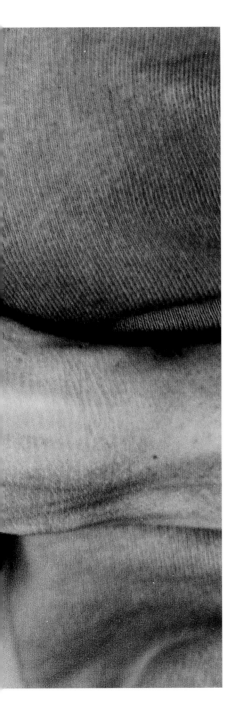

25.01.2000 ciara's shoe, falls creek, australia

and opens a website. Finds herself unavailable to run in her shoe company's favourite meet in Eugene, Oregon, so suggests a road race in Holland to call it quits. Okey dokey.

Reebok were generous in exchange for her face, her body and a few days a year of her time. Companies sensed stardom and hitched a ride. Things were set up so that when the bad years came they didn't hit her financially.

The portfolio changed. Of course. In the process of ransacking her life after 1997 she converted to the church of Nike. Her Reebok contract had ended twelve months previously and Reebok were spring cleaning anyway. Nike were offering something, which felt like a new start.

Happy chance. Nike's deal was based on bonuses and the World Cross Country double and European double of 1998 brought her back to better than normal again. "What I would have saved for 10 years time maybe. I'll notice then perhaps. It doesn't cost too much to live now though."

When she won the World Cross Country Championship they flew her out to Nike's headquarters in Beaverton, Oregon and there was a big banner up across the campus: 'Welcome Sonia O'Sullivan - World Cross Country Champion.'

It struck her then but, not for the first time, she was enjoying this windfall of glory more than she had enjoyed anything in her spangled career. She sat back and savoured this life flavoured by success and money.

You've come a long way girl, she thought.

11.05.2000 end of training run, sandymount strand, dublin, ireland

27.01.2000 training diary, falls creek, australia

23.04.2000 balmoral, scotland

27.01.2000 langford's gap, falls creek, australia

standing still

Sydney fills the windscreen. Atlanta grows smaller in the rear-view mirror.

Finally.

She never went back to the stadium again and when she remembers the place it is as a cauldron. She remembers the black interior, the Olympic flame looking like a McDonalds logo. She remembers leaving the place for the last time, just looking for an exit that would discreetly consume her. Mostly she doesn't remember it at all.

There is a lady, Angela Barker, living up the road who gives her massages and on her wall she has postcards from all over the world. Sonia's eyes invariably fall on the one from Atlanta. Every time she sees it her head conjures up the image of fire.

"When I think of it that's how I feel. It was a cauldron and I was just glad to get out of there. No happy memories of the place."

If you want to know, yes, it can be lonely. People stick around on the bad days but they are fewer and they are muted.

Around winners everything is clamorous and well lit as a fairground. Being busy engulfs you. Everyone wants the benediction of your words, the favour of your time. When it stops, everything diminishes. The colour drains away. Cooking dinner and doing washing and making tea. All those things loom again. Mountains in your day. You notice you are doing them again.

After Atlanta she scarcely spoke. She reckons she cried every night for two weeks. She'd spend time with people and turn the dimmer button behind her eyes up just enough to convince them she was okay. By night she'd be miserable. Miserable and alone most of the time. So frustrated and annoyed and unable to figure things out.

People wanted answers. Theories developed in hothouse imaginations. It's impossible that this happened, there must have been something in her breakfast cereal which turned her into a bad athlete. Everyone had their quack theories and explanations. Doctors and psychologists were writing to the papers. One big free for all.

A friend told her that mercury fillings were the cause. They steal the energy from you. So she got them out pronto. Changed them all. Went to the dentist every week for a while. He even took out the wisdom teeth as part of the bargain.

She saw all kinds of doctors, signed up for every kind of blood test.

"It got to the point where I wasn't really looking for answers. I was just looking for a way forward."

She never wanted to believe after Atlanta that she'd done anything wrong. Still doesn't. She'd thought everything was right. She went as the raging favourite. Came back as the pre-eminent casualty.

She'd pictured happy endings. She'd go. They'd hand her the gold medal. They'd say: Sonia, this is yours. Take it. You've earned it. Happy ever after.

Anatomy of a calamity: It wasn't the right time? She just couldn't do it? She didn't take the chance? Things just went wrong? She overtrained? She ran out of energy? She caught a urinary tract infection? Whatever. The Games were gone. The world was moving on. She was stuck. Eventually she told herself that the video was downstairs, she was never going to look at it, never going to change it.

Still. Kim McDonald had entered her name in the usual slew of races for the rest of the year. McDonald would call, leaving messages asking Sonia to decide what she would be doing and she was, in her own words, just ignoring him.

The following year compounded the misery and marked a new beginning. It was one of those years when there was a hint that she'd be as good as she had been before. She had a chance to win a medal at the World Championships and a chance of getting beaten up again.

She ran well in the heats and semi-finals of the 1500 but the 3rd race was just one race too many for her. The week crumbled in familiar fashion. This time though her life didn't go with it. She'd begun working with Alan Storey, a new coach introduced to her at the World Cross Country Championships that spring. She'd gone there bereft of direction and come back with a new coach. Good enough. Maybe the comeback began then. Maybe earlier.

26.01.2000 falls creek, australia

Late in 1996 Nick Bideau had arrived. Former partner and manager of Cathy Freeman the Australian icon. At the end of 1997 before the end of the track season with races still going on, they'd escaped to Sicily and the streets of cobblestone which prohibited running. They went to the pool, swam in the sea, ate and drank what they liked. Except for the pink Italian sports papers, they lost touch with the world of running.

"I wouldn't want to change anything. They were all experiences that I went through, some good things, some bad things but I'm not sure if I hadn't done it that I'd still be here and still be as good as I am, as interested as I am. Atlanta and Athens, they were parts of the path.

Eventually I ran in Edinburgh that October. It was a 5K road race against Yvonne Murray and I think she was second and I was first. Just being able to do something like that gave me the energy to get back into things. I said to myself that I'm moving on now, I'll do some new things. I sort of realised then that I was the last person in the world left thinking about it all."

24.06.2000 gare du nord, paris, france

24.01.2000 falls creek, australia

19.07.2000 at home with nick, east molsley, surrey, england

16.05.2000 at home with ciara

eyeballs out

It was in Falls Creek in 1998 when she finally decided that whatever Alan Storey said was what she would do.

"It's not eyeballs out," he will say, and she will ease off a fraction.

She'd seen the nature of obsession. Back in 1995 and 1996 she had a computer programme. She would come in from training and key in all the details of the session just passed. The computer would whirr and tell her everything, average pace per mile, per kilometre and so on. Every detail.

She calls it the ABC business. Agent, boyfriend and coach. At one stage they were all the one. Three persons in the one Kim. Sonia and Kim. Nick Bideau and Cathy Freeman. These multi-function relationships never come apart easily. Ties are hacked away with a butter knife.

It's not always easy to keep the roles separate. Even now Nick is an agent and manager to a slew of athletes and they live in a house where track times and split times and meet schedules are the lingua franca. There's overlap. Nick coaches, so he knows bits and pieces about everything that's going on. Sometimes he can't help himself but think aloud. So now she waits 'till she's going out the door before she mentions what sort of session she is headed for. Sometimes the ABC business is distracting. Nick and Alan clashed strongly a couple of times on the road to Sydney. In Villamoura, Alan felt it best that Sonia just run the shorter of the two cross-country races. Nick felt otherwise.

09.07.2000 nice, france

After London they disagreed about the training session imposed the Tuesday before. Nick felt that Sonia had lost her last chance at a confidence-building 5000 metres race. Alan felt that everything was subservient to the goal of getting to Sydney in the best possible shape.

"The best shape mentally as well as physically," countered Nick.

By and large though, the roles are separate and distinct. Often Nick will say to Sonia, "you have to talk to Alan about that and talk to him on your own. I can't be involved." Often she'll tell him the same thing.

That's how it has to be. Can't eat track 24/7. Not any longer.

She remembers some sessions she and Kim would devise. They'd plan for weeks in advance and the sessions became events in themselves, they became bigger than races for her 'till in the end she'd actually get nervous beforehand. The intensity built and built all the way to Atlanta, the two of them just pushing the envelope until it burst. Something had to give.

What worked for a long time got to be too much. Too repetitive, too much athletics. All running, all the time. After 1996, in that storm of pure unhappiness, things were going to change.

"I had to separate everything straight away. In 1997, I even went through a stage where Kim was representing me but I wouldn't speak to him. He said I went out of my way to run every possible race that I had never run before just going to places where he didn't have a good relationship with the organisers. I didn't really. It was just part of the independence thing. I picked out certain races, the right ones for me and it amounted to a radical change.

After Atlanta was when I decided that I couldn't have Kim coaching me any longer. If I was getting stressed out about training it was time to stop. Sometimes he wouldn't tell me what I was doing 'till I got to the track. Sometimes a session would be looming in my head for weeks."

"It's not eyeballs out," Alan will say.

Not anymore.

79

19.07.2000 east molsley, surrey, england

down under

E-Mail from Sonia O' Sullivan: "We've arrived. It's 5am. We're freezing."

Word from Nick Bideau: "I told you so."

In Melbourne on a Friday in early September she wraps up four years of work. She begins to tidy her affairs and wind down for the Olympics. Four years of putting herself back together again. Four years since she came home from Atlanta neatly dismantled and with some parts lost in transit.

There's been misery. Athens. Turin. Lots of races she couldn't win and lots of races she just didn't want to be in. There was the sundering with Kim McDonald. A time of bewildering loneliness.

And there was recovery. Falling in love with Nick Bideau. Meeting Alan Storey. Double World Cross Country Championships in Morocco. Double European Championships in Budapest. Ciara's arrival. Sonia finding a way to live with a love of running but not quite an obsession with it.

Four years. She takes her last really long run before the Games here in Melbourne, a relaxed ninety minute canter down along the Albert Park lake, up towards the Yarra River and north Melbourne, striding onwards then to the city's famous track, The Tan, a dusty loop which takes runners four kilometres around the fragrant botanical gardens. The air is bracing. Clears the head.

Four years and now the last serious work before the Games. The final tidying. Last cobwebs brushed away. Everything afterwards will be countdown.

They stay for a week in a suite hotel in Melbourne before heading north to Couran Cove, on Australia's Gold Coast.

There it's perfect. They stay in Ron Clarke's villa. Sonia, Nick, Ciara and Sandy Richards, the Jamaican 400 metre runner.

At Couran Cove there are Swiss, Germans and South Africans out training for the Games. Anytime she goes out for a run she sees the famous and familiar faces.

Her final races are in Runaway Bay. A good hard 800 metres and then as an afterthought, pushing herself a little too hard by competing in the 1500 when the afternoon has gone cold and windy.

She wins the second race but pays the price on Tuesday. She goes training but doesn't feel too good. She's only been in Australia ten days after all. She starts the session proposing to do six laps at seventy second pace. Quick but not as quick as hoped for. It is late, dark and windy.

She's tough but she's tired. She's crunching her gears, grinding her teeth. Does 3x300s. Calls it a night. Not a great night.

urine, blood & needles

A strand, a sample even, from the theme of the Games.

Sonia hears the Chinese woman coming all huffy puffy down the track beside her. She notices her grimace. She's holding her side and gasping for breath like a woman for whom the air has turned to water. Sonia notes her distress and wants no share in such bad karma. She moves on. Three days later, the same Chinese woman breezes through the 10,000 final. One long swoosh. She's just nineteen, the only one of Ma Junren's runners to make it to Sydney. She runs like a dream.

And it makes you wonder. Even Sonia, who gave up wondering a long time ago.

When she talks about drugs in her workplace the anger doesn't punch out from inside her chest. The rage isn't there anymore. Can't afford it. She needs the energy too much. She works in a world where the innocence has been pilfered and the greatest heroes are the biggest suspects. She just looks after her side of the street now.

She accepted long ago that she can't police the business and that good runners gossip themselves into mediocrity wondering about what fuels great runners.

What she can do is run on her record, a world class runner since she was a kid, run on her associates: from Sean Kennedy, to Kim McDonald to Alan Storey to Nick Bideau and through dozens of training partners, people so squeaky clean that there hasn't been so much as a whisper. She runs on her openness, her "come and watch me train" transparency. In a trade where nobody trusts anyone, it has to be enough.

The hard line according to Sonia:

"I know I'm not cheating. I have never cheated. I never would. That leaves me having to get the best out of myself with what I have got. There isn't really anything I can do about the people who are cheating. There seems to be such a lack of proof, the good guys are always behind. The cheaters are one step ahead. If I took drugs and I had a positive drugs test I'd have to go and live on a desert island somewhere. I couldn't live with it. So many athletes aren't the focus of attention in their country. They get caught and other people take their place and nobody cares but I'm running in Sydney and I can hear Irish people calling my name, see them waving the flags. People would never forgive me. I can't imagine that attention, the reactions, what my father would say to me. It's different being from Ireland than it is being from anywhere else. Everything that Ireland has given me. You can't even think of it."

She used to wonder. Now she lets life unfold. You bet she used to wonder. Tetyana Dorovskikh the silver medallist from her Olympic final in Barcelona tested positive for steroids the following summer. The Chinese wonders of Ma Junren just shrugged their shoulders and walked away from Sydney when they heard about the EPO testing which would be imposed upon them.

Add it up and probably she's owed an Olympic bronze from Barcelona and two World Championship golds from Stuttgart. A woman could go mad if she wanted to play detective.

"I heard about the Chinese this time and there was some anger in me. I thought straight away, why did it take seven years to admit this? It makes you wonder are there tests being done and are people's positives really being revealed. Usually though, I don't get involved in all that talk. It goes on but it gives you one more thing to spend energy on."

Set against the rumours and scandals there's the sheer ordinariness of working life. She can hardly imagine the murk around her. People talk about drugs all the time but she's never seen drugs, never been offered drugs, wouldn't know what to do with drugs. They talk about finding syringe needle boxes in the Olympic village. She shivers at the mention.

19.09.2000 sandy beach, botany bay, sydney, australia

"I've never stuck a needle into myself in my life. I go for a blood test every month and I cringe before the needle is taken out of the packet."

For a clean athlete, the random tests are a frustration more than a deterrent.

With the system in such disrepute, the reason for not doping has to be a little more profound than fear of getting caught. "You don't do it because you want to see what you've got in yourself. You want to push yourself and know what you can do. You want to enjoy your achievements."

She got tested at nearly every Grand Prix meet this year. Always testing her, she reckons because she'd come back after a year off, a year outside the system.

It gets irritating even if you're on the side of the angels.

"You're thinking, 'I'm clean', why aren't you out getting somebody else?"

"After the 5000 metres final in Sydney, they hadn't even got a cubicle ready to take the urine sample in. They know what the schedule is and you say to them can we do this now and they don't have a cubicle ready. It doesn't make you confident in them."

She admires her friend Paula Radcliffe for wearing the ribbons that demand blood testing at the track but...

"I agree with her but will Paula ever change it? I want blood tests but I think if you come out once on the drugs issue people want you to talk about it always. I've got to focus on racing. I suppose I just assume that if you are clean people expect you'd be in favour of blood testing."

So, she lives the life she loves and loves the life she lives. Drugs are out there somewhere and she has a last thought. If you're a clean athlete somebody has to be out there standing up for you and doing the work for you. You can't stick a dagger into every back that passes you in a race. Next question?

she lives on scott street

Scott Street is in Mortdale, a sleepy suburb of Sydney. Number 15a is Sonia Central for the Olympics.

She arrives in Sydney on Friday and goes straight from the airport to the Olympic Village where she stays until after the opening ceremony. The village is fine but it's bright and noisy too early in the morning. Noisy too late at night also.

Nick goes to Scott Street. She calls him next morning.

"Well?"

He lists every possible defect, every drawback. From the soft beds to the giant bible near the telly.

She arrives to inspect. Deems the garden perfect for Ciara, the shade perfect for herself. The place is surrounded by parks. And beaches. Indeed there's a perfect poem worth of coves and bays: Jew Fish. Gungah. Lime Kiln. Boggywell.

She runs for twenty three minutes around Olds Park in the mornings. Does her stretches and sit-ups. Finds ducks to feed and beaches to walk with Ciara in the afternoons.

Somewhere out there, the Olympics are going on.

ciara

"Now," says Sonia in Scott Street, "we have to do some Ciara things." And she swoops down and picks her daughter up and carries her through the air.

Nothing but the sound of giggles. Two sets.

This happy baby has celebrated one birthday. Been places and seen things that you never dreamed of.

This year: England. Ireland. Scotland. France. Italy. Australia. Belgium. Singapore. Qatar. Switzerland. USA. Norway. Bahrain. Portugal.

Here's a moment. Villamoura, Portugal, the World Cross Country Championships are over. Greg Allen of RTE is interviewing Sonia. He is a meticulous questioner, a trait Sonia respects but doesn't always enjoy.

Today she feels the interview is going on for longer than she feels it should. She's itching to be away, to see Nick and Ciara. Greg Allen asks a question and the inference Sonia draws from it is that she isn't running well because of Ciara.

"It just seemed over the line to me. It touched on me. It was the greatest thing for me to be there with Ciara and I'm having to consider that if Ciara wasn't there, would I have won? I wouldn't let that be a consideration. If she wasn't there maybe I wouldn't have been there. Yet I'm here in Portugal. I've come seventh. It was tough but I ran as well as I had in Marrakech. I needed a break from Greg. I'd had enough. Asking about Ciara was enough."

And she turned away in tears.

19.09.2000 sandy beach, botany bay, sydney, australia

backstory

Sydney: Tuesday afternoon in Scott Street, and Sonia is chasing Ciara in the garden. The Olympic 5000 metre heats are three days away. Six days to go to the final. The sky is blue and clear. The people sitting in the shade are relaxed.

"Has Marie-Jo Perec dropped out of the 400 metres yet?" says Nick Bideau.

"No."

"She will," he says, "she will."

Fast forward. Six nights later. Sonia is at doping control. She has a silver medal in her pocket. Nick is jouncing Ciara in his arms. Marie-Jo Perec has been back in France for three days.

One question dropped into the pool of celebration. "How did you know Marie-Jo was going to drop out?" Nick Bideau needs no pause.

"I spent years, years mate, years looking into Marie-Jo's head. I know how she thinks. I knew she'd get here and couldn't face the possibility of being beaten. I knew she'd go rather than lose."

And he looks over your shoulder to the monitor behind you. There, Cathy Freeman is winning the 400 metres Olympic Final for the hundredth time tonight. For Nick Bideau however, this is the first time he has watched the moment. All those years planning and now it's a replay before he sees it. In the wash of Sonia's silver an Australian journalist has hollered the inevitable question: What did you think of Cathy's race?

"Didn't see it," he replied curtly.

Now he watches the slo-mo with an analyst's eye.

"Aw. Look at her stride. All over the place at the end. Perec might be sorry she missed that."

Cathy Freeman comes home unchallenged for the glory of Australia yet again. Nick Bideau turns his head away from the clamorous glory of the woman he once loved, tutored and virtually made. He talks about splits and the personal bests for a minute or so, a ticker tape of stats on what is an oddly confusing night. Then:

"Cathy's family hugged me and thanked me," he says. "That was nice."

And his head returns to the business of Sonia and whatever is detaining her at doping control.

If only these things came apart cleanly. Sonia and Kim McDonald fell away from each other, leaving wounds unstitched. Nick Bideau and Cathy Freeman used a butter knife to hack away at the ties.

A quick primer on Nick Bideau and Cathy Freeman: They met. They fell in love, a relationship based on shared obsession. For outsiders it was Pygmalion with spikes. She was young from Koori. He was crowding early middle age, from Melbourne. He had the ideas. She had the legs.

The obsession, the relentless, suffocating humidity of it broke them up in the end. Nick met Sonia. Cathy met Sandy Bodecker, a middle-aged Nike executive clinging to surf boy looks.

Nick continued to be Cathy Freeman's business partner, continued to unfold his long-term plan for her success. It worked for a while. Then in May 2000, at the gate to the Games almost, Cathy Freeman cut Nick Bideau loose.

It hurt him. It outraged him. He was sorry he hadn't beaten her to the punch and he was troubled that the last page of a plan almost a decade in the making was going to be executed without him. He'd plotted every step. Booked the races, the flights, the hotels, played the mind Games. In 1996 when Freeman had lost to Perec in the Olympic final he'd told her that Sydney would be her time. To make sure of that, she had to choose a venue and beat Perec there by the end of the year. She did. They started messing with Perec's head again.

Yet Nick Bideau and Cathy Freeman got to court before they got to the Olympics. Battery acid words were splashed around. The media piled in on the side of the national icon. To necklace just two insults together, Bideau was a "unaustralian traitor." It was alleged that Cathy Freeman had gone cross-eyed crazy upon learning of Sonia's pregnancy.

The case was suspended in early July leaving the emotions and anger undetonated. The needling rolled on all the way to Homebush Bay and for those around Sonia O' Sullivan, the darling of Australia, Cathy Freeman, became a little spoken of, almost comical figure mentioned only as "she who must not be mentioned."

"We shot Bambi," says Peter Jess, business partner to Nick Bideau. "RUN!"

For Sonia there were tandem needs. She needed to avoid distraction. She wanted to support Nick.

"It was hard at first but ever since he stopped working with her it was fine. I never got involved in it, not all the stuff through the summer. A couple of times he was bothered and I knew it. I'd ask him and he'd say you really don't want to know. Maybe when we would be out on a run he'd tell me a few bits and pieces to give me some idea. I'd tell him it didn't matter what it says in the papers. I'm here for you and Ciara is here, so what does it matter?" Things matter though. For Nick Bideau it was business, career and self-esteem. For Sonia it was more eggshell delicate.

"It got to me a little. I always get the paper. Then I saw something. I can't remember what it was and then I couldn't buy a newspaper. I knew people had written this stuff that wasn't true and I was thinking maybe it's all made up. People are siding with one person. Why am I wasting my time on this?"

She missed every last detail being dredged and sifted. The news of Cathy Freeman going cross eyed crazy when she heard of Sonia's pregnancy. Word from Ireland that it was in the paper that Freeman had allegedly described Sonia as "the devil."

"I never knew that. First I heard was that my mother called and said it was in the paper in Ireland."

Mary O' Sullivan called one Sunday adjacent to the Games, the sheaves of crisp newspaper rattling down the phone.

"Do you know what she said?" "No." "Will I read it to you?" "No I don't want to know."

"Just this bit?" "No." "She says..."

Does all this matter?

Well, the black joke of the Olympic schedule puts Cathy Freeman's 400 metres final and Sonia O'Sullivan's 5000 metre final on stage within an hour of each other. It supplies an unlikely personal tension to the night. Where exactly will their paths intersect?

Rewind. It's late on the same Tuesday afternoon in Sydney. Hands in pockets, Sonia strolls along the shade pools and dappled coves by Botany Bay. Ciara is dabbling soft feet in the greeny shallows. There is the shuffle of sand between Sonia's toes. She's walking and considering the imminent future.

You want to ask her: Does all this back-story matter?

But her face has that 'top of the straight and one hundred to go' fierceness right now and you know the answer already. Cathy Freeman could live on a different planet than this. Sonia has bigger thoughts to fry.

26.09.2000 "...only one race in sydney last night"

blondie

How long ago is it now? Helsinki. Six years ago perhaps. She came third in the Euro champs in 1994. Sonia won. Yvonne Murray came second.

Gabriela Szabo. In 1995 she ran the World Championships in Gothenburg like a kid. Really fast for one lap. Then they caught her and ate her. Sonia got gold again.

Those early times left Szabo with a fear. Take Zurich in 1995 when Sonia ran an 8:27 for the 3000 metres. Szabo took the lead on the back straight and thought for a while that she'd cracked it. Round the bend with the crowd in her ears and Sonia strode by insouciant and brilliant. Invincible then.

They've never been friends. Never liked each other very much. All those years on the circuit and they'd never run together, never make an effort to get over the language difficulties.

"When I was beating her," says Sonia, "she was like a bear."

When she stopped beating, her the relationship retained that soreness.

In 1998, at the end of a perfect summer, Sonia went to Berlin and lost a fast 5000 metre race to Szabo. Szabo, beaten badly by Sonia in the European finals, hadn't been so much as acknowledging Sonia all summer. Losing in Berlin hurt badly enough to bring tears.

That was then.

There's a briny sunshine over Couran Cove today as Sonia waits for the ferry. She, Nick Sandy Richards and Ciara are on the ferry. Fifteen minutes from mainland to island. They are sitting on the deck area, having coffee.

Nick says, "Hey, look over there."

Over there are the ghostly, prim features of Gabriela Szabo. Sonia starts laughing impulsively as eyes meet. The two runners exchange weak waves across the deck area. Sandy Richards begins making jokes and speaking loudly. Soon they are all laughing happily and loud as partiers in the Great Gatsby. The boat cuts on through the water. Szabo watches.

Two days later at the track. Szabo is there. Anita Weyermann of Switzerland too. Sonia is used to Tuesday nights with the Thames Hares and Hounds. Now she's got people training around her who she will race against. Rivals on either side of her.

She makes a decision.

"I had a feeling I was going to do something fast. Alan asked me what I wanted to do. I pulled out a session that would give me some confidence. The slowest things in there were some 400 metre runs at 60 seconds each."

So Gabriela Szabo spent an age warming up and all the while Sonia whistled past her like a bullet nicking her ear.

Felt good. She asked Nick later what Szabo had been doing. "Some four hundreds, some two hundreds. Hard to tell. I was watching you."

Leaving Couran Cove. Migrating to the Olympics. Sonia, Nick and Ciara on deck again. Ciara does an old trick. Tugs the hair of the person in front. Gabriela Szabo's husband/coach turns around. Szabo turns too, sees Ciara and melts into a smile.

The cold war ends.

one giant footstep

Friday. First night of the athletics in Homebush. This beautiful stadium nurtures all ambitions for the moment. Sonia's heat is the first of the two. She reduces the race to routine. Finishes first. Fastest qualifier. Has she broken sweat even?

Ah! This was the girl we once knew. Same old battler. She destroys the field without looking back. Comes to the mixed zone and puts order on the media.

Three minutes here. Ok? Just a minute there? Ok?

She hoicks up her too large tracksuit and whisks herself away. Have to warm down she says with a smile. She knows it's back. Whatever went away. It's back.

Pressure is for bicycle tyres, you think.

Easy rests the head.

adidas

IRELAND

Sydney 2000

2155

five

Her night. This is her night.

She leans forward slightly on the starting line, her face illumined by excitement and expectation. A thousand times she's known this posture and these feelings. Her ears strain in case she misses the gun through the din of the people watching the pole vault. She balls her fists, samples the lightness of herself on her toes, feels the breath of 112,000 people on her neck.

You think about a day, a certain day for years and years before it happens. And then it dawns without thunderclaps or heralding angels. It comes as cups of coffee and fresh newspapers and feeding Ciara. It comes as softball on the television and your favourite restaurant not open for lunch. You wonder: Why hasn't the world stopped turning? This is my day.

Finally she packs up her bag. Same old routine but it takes ten checks and ten re-checks. She's allocated a corner of Scott Street for all her Irish gear. Still she's jumpy.

Checklist: Number. Yeah. Spikes. Yeah. Drink. Yeah. Tracksuit. Yeah. Singlet. Yeah. Shorts. Yeah.

And that's it. You'd fit the tools of her trade into your pocket if you had a mind to.

They get into the red landcrawler at five. Sonia, Nick, Alan and Ciara off to the Olympics. There's a sense of tension, a sense of adventure, a sense of nappy needing changing.

Nick drives to the village. Conversation is airy and light. Sonia gets out at the Olympic village and the big red vehicle trundles off to find parking at the Nike offices. Alone at last.

She gets a coffee, tries to read the village newspaper, finds herself surprisingly calm. She'd been jumpy on Friday before the heats, like a demon on Thursday the day before the heats. Now she's herself. Cup of coffee, a scone, a read. Puts down the minutes like an assassin waiting.

Through the village. Meets Irish team manager Patsy McGonagle. They catch a bus from one end of the village to the other and then catch another bus to the stadium.

She's in real time now that she can hear the crowd. She's counted down these minutes in her head already. Got there at seven. Race is five to nine and the check in forty minutes earlier, so that's 8:15 you check in so you want to begin warming up at ten to eight. Time to relax a bit before that, lie down, put the feet up in the air and read a magazine.

She decides to take about ten minutes when she won't read anything. Just think. Think Sonia. Clear everything out of your mind. She lies down, legs in the air. Thinks of bad times and good. Thinks of whom she owes this to.

So many people. Thinks until her mind is pleasantly uncluttered. Her feet are high above her. She doesn't know why she props them up there but she's done it since she won the World Student Games in 1991 and it's a comforter. She's just lying there, all quiet and still when she hears the familiar excited squealing. Ciara.

She jumps up, every worry erased. Plays for a little in the infield with her daughter 'till it's time to say goodbye. Her Dad, John O'Sullivan comes in to say hello, to say he loves her. Time is pressing on them now. He goes quickly.

Around ten to eight she walks a lap of the track with Alan Storey, the pair of them in the surrendering light talking about what she is going to do. Keep up. Mainly that's it. Keep up.

"It will be consistently hard for the whole race," Alan says. "Keep up. Remind yourself that there'll be hard times in the race. Watch for gaps opening up. Be stubborn. Fight."

It's tough to figure out anything more. Sonia has most respect for Gete Wami and the two other Ethiopians, then the three Kenyans. Then there's the ghostly Szabo.

She's finishing her warm up when the warm up track tannoy crackles.

Incredibly, Cathy Freeman's 400 metre final is being broadcast live to athletes warming up for their own events.

The volume is too high for clarity, yet she has to smile at the irony of it.

She who shall not be mentioned has invaded the sacred time before Sonia's race.

Sonia surmises from the rising clamour what is happening.

"It just got noisier and noisier. You knew then. Otherwise you'd have heard a pin drop. I just went on with it."

Time. She goes to the call room. Relaxed as a cat in the sun. Now it's routine. When to jog, when to stretch and relax. The old familiar. People are sprinting up and down this tiny room, nervy and pale. She writes them off. On the other side of the tunnel there's a bit of track to run up and down, they must know that. A group of runners gather around the television now to watch the men's 400 metres final. Sonia has to ask later who won it.

She exchanges smiles and eye contact with Jo Pavey of Britain. No talk.

Nice when there are people in there that you have a connection with. Makes you feel more comfortable.

The field for the women's 5000 metres final come out of the call room and down the tunnel. Ten years of these big races and every time the woman leading the racers out walks slowly as if leading athletes to their death but this one time it gets hot tin roof jumpy.

Gabriela Szabo starts jogging. Somebody else starts. Suddenly everyone is jogging, including the official who is leading the athletes over. Sonia wants to walk but she has to walk quickly. The athletes look like an army platoon now running along with knapsacks on their backs. Sonia is laughing, jogging a bit, walking fast for a bit, thinking this is the most ridiculous moment of her life. Then they burst out into the stadium and she leaves those thoughts behind.

Officials move among the athletes now doing the last minute stuff. They take everyone's accreditation tags away, check the vest numbers, give the runners numbers to stick on their hips. Everyone changes into their spikes, puts their gear in baskets, sucks in the cool air. Sonia, as ever, folds her gear precisely. Lays it down neatly and then resumes her strides. There's meeting and greeting to be done too. She does her waving early, acknowledging the tricolours, the Irish voices, getting rid of the pressure by not thinking of the pressure.

Then time compresses. They are summoned to the line and their faces loom one by one on the big screen in Homebush and on small screens in almost every corner of the world. "And reigning European Champion, Sonia O' Sullivan." Small wave. Stiff smile. Twelve and a half laps of work ahead.

By lap four you are thinking that her day is over and her time has gone.

Her face is tight and glowing with sweat. Her legs are heavy, thumping the ground as she falls back through the field. For two laps or more her face is a postcard from Atlanta 1996.

Help comes not from nearly two decades of running but from one of the last things to enter her head. She bought a book the other day. Shopping for distractions when her eye landed on Winning Attitudes edited by Herb Elliott, the old Aussie icon. Upbeat thoughts for dipping into when the hours dragged by. All those winning formulae herded between two covers. She thought she might cadge one.

Like a charm it works and the leg irons fall away.

"There was a bit in the book about the voice inside you. The voice that says 'do you want to do this?' What are you going to say?"

Yes.

Stubbornly she hangs on to the back of Jo Pavey. The pace ahead slows. She wedges herself between a couple of Kenyans. Then she gets caught in the current of the Ethiopians. Normal service resumes in her legs.

Into the business time now. They've been laggardly through the 3000 metre mark. The final five laps are up-tempo craziness. Suddenly Wami is haranguing the other Ethiopians. Legs pumping, elbows flying. Shouting. Make your mind up. C'mon. The Ethiopians can't do anything. Wami is irritated. She can't get free. The race is a flat out lung buster now.

No guts, no glory, says Sonia to herself. Just increase the braveness. Lay it out there girl.

Homebush Bay is alight now. This race has suddenly gone off like an express train. Sonia O'Sullivan has no right to be up there. Tonight she has no choice but to be up there. The music gets faster and faster.

"We were going so fast that they couldn't have gone any faster. In the last four laps it felt so easy. Keeping up was easy. Early on when I got detached I struggled. When I got back I thought that I had been given a second chance. I couldn't lose it again."

She is lost in it. Like she hasn't been for years. No idea of lap times. No sense of the blurry crowds. Just the crazy rhythm. She watches Wami. She watches Szabo.

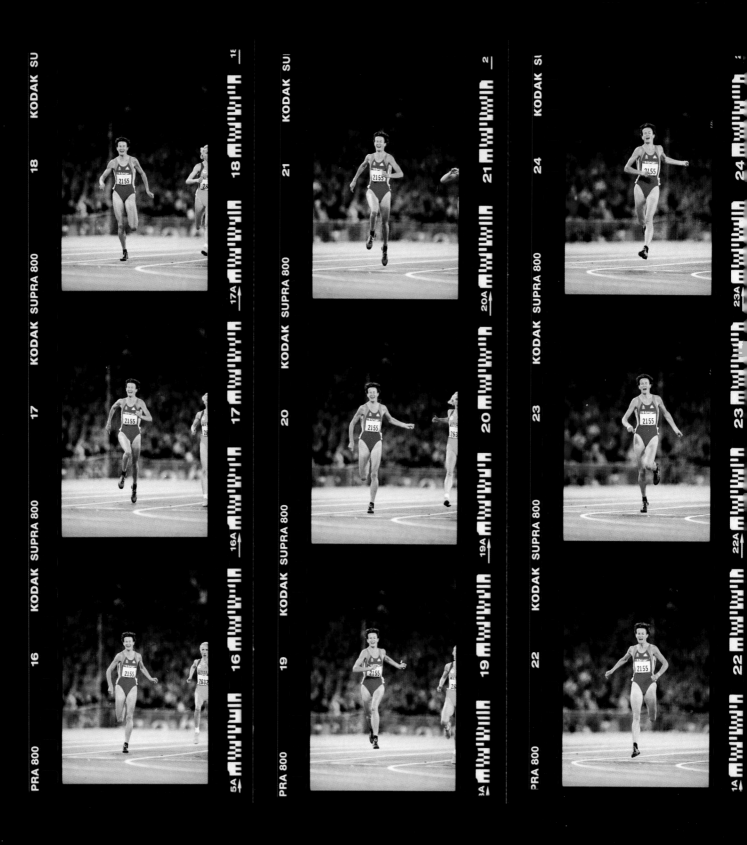

"I was waiting for as long as possible. Going down the back straight I thought maybe this is it. The German girl went. Szabo and I went after her. Stopped that. After that I wasn't aware of what was behind."

Coming off the bend. Blood rushing in the head. Heart jumping. Tight brown stomach heaving. She's close to winning. So close it almost jars her.

Gabriela Szabo has gone , half-fearing Sonia's kick. Here it comes.

Sonia feels bigger, stronger, faster on the way home but Szabo has the inside line and a fractional advantage. Szabo has a little trick she uses too. Twice as they shift off the bend her elbows do a little shuffle. It's a mite distracting and it gives the impression that suddenly she has shifted gear and is running faster. It buys milliseconds.

Look at them now. Szabo, small and wan. Sonia, tall and lithe. Twenty eight seconds down this last two hundred metres, feet skimming this earth. They cross the line leaving their hearts and souls spent and smeared on the track behind them. Szabo spreads her arms wide. Sonia throws her head up.

"So close," she says, "so close."

Two thoughts arrive before she recovers. She has lost a race. Even in training, even the last run of a lazy night she hates to lose. Yet, yet, yet. Her mind can process that she has a medal, that she has run a wonderful race with a crazy finish. She's no longer at war with herself. All the old certainties are back.

Nick and Ciara materialise from nowhere for the second time today. The three of them stand in a tight knot, arms around each other and Sonia O'Sullivan sheds her first tear of these happy Olympics. She's found the missing part of herself.

PS: Afterwards paths kept intersecting. There are no etiquette guides to help with these situations. Sonia brandished the cult hero of the Games for the pleasure of the masses.

Viva Fatso, the Fat Arsed Wombat! She took a lap of honour to thank the tricolours. She was absorbing her moment just as Cathy Freeman was presented with her medal.

Coming off the final bend Sonia had a choice. Make a run down the straight and finish the lap of honour quickly or dawdle and stand to attention as Advance Australia Fair is played and the Southern Cross is raised.

She opts for that part of discretion which survives when you sprint down the straight with your national flag streaming and your friends harrooing, just as the woman who put horns and cloven feet on you gets a gold medal. Call it a draw.

after five

The doorbell sounds early next morning. It wakes nobody. Sonia has had one beer. Got to bed at 3am. Got up at 3:20am. Taken a sleeping pill.

Stirred again when she heard Ciara gurgling in the morning.

The television people are here. So is Pat Hickey, Ireland IOC member. The crew film a live interview with Sonia while Pat Hickey moves about in the background and a nation wonders if he isn't part of the housekeeping staff here.

The TV people evaporate. So does Pat Hickey. Alan Storey decides to take Ciara out for a walk while Nick and Sonia go for a run. They all leave. It starts to rain.

Everyone is back in Scott Street. Sonia. Nick. Ciara. Alan. Peter Jess. John O' Sullivan. Sonia has a press conference in Nike at 2pm.

Supposed to meet the Minister for Sport sometime between three and four. Then to the Irish Olympic house at 8pm. Sonia is tired. The Minister and the revellers at the Olympic house have no chance of seeing her.

She reads the papers. All Cathy Freeman all the time.

"Only one race in Sydney last night," she says, not bitterly.

Nick views the same pages more carefully. He was part of this story too, one of the creators of it but he has suppressed it for Sonia's sake. It's a strange morning after feel.

Around mid-day Sonia and Alan Storey go out into the house extension with the utility room and bathroom. Sonia is inclined to do the 10,000 metres. Alan doesn't think so. After this conversation Nick is sore at Alan for inserting a reed of doubt in Sonia's mind. Not for the first time things are tense between them.

Sonia says: "Suppose I run the heats tomorrow and if I feel bad I won't go in the final." Silence. She adds: "Can you do that?" Alan says: "I don't know. Can YOU do it?"

They come back into the main house. Each knowing that Sonia will run the 10,000, that wild horses wouldn't have stopped her. The whole point of the night before hasn't been the silver medal, but the end of the journey, the completion of the rehabilitation.

Sonia is happy again. Happy and headstrong. Can't look at a race without wanting to be in it.

25.09.2000 sonia, silver and fatso the fat arsed wombat.

ten

Here's where the story ends...

The last night of fun and games at Homebush opens with the women's 10,000 metres final. The race just gets away from Sonia O'Sullivan, slips out of her hand like a caught fish. There. Gone.

Five runners make a break and Sonia O'Sullivan never closes the gap. She owns sixth place forever.

She thinks of quitting but she hears people calling her name. Go on girl. She's kind of surprised. She wants to stop and tell people that the bunch are so far off it's impossible to catch up. Impossible.

She's alone out there. The bunch ahead. The stragglers behind. Thoughts are loud in her head.

"I don't want to have to explain this," she says. "Not to Alan. Or Nick. Even to Ciara sometime. Don't want to explain it to myself. I was in an Olympic final and I didn't do my best? If I finish fifteenth and off the pace so far that I jog the last lap I didn't want to have to explain it. I came here ready to win, was ready to win. Now I'm in the best women's 10,000 race ever held. I owe something here."

For a while she thought maybe she would catch up. She tried for about five laps of maybe and perhaps and somehow. Somebody will drop off maybe and I'll catch up with them.

A few of us will chase them down perhaps, do it as a group. They'll just slow down. Somehow or other they'll come back to me.

In your dreams Sonia, says the race, in your dreams.

30.09.2000 start line 10,000 metres final

She's listening to its words. She's loving this place. Seventy yards off where she wants to be, but, hey, an Olympic final and she's whole again.

"There's more to being here than the medals," she says, "there's more to running than winning, there's just the rhythm of it."

The red skinned track keeps disappearing beneath her spikes. Those Irish voices pierce her head so cleanly now that she can discern the region the accents belong to.

Go on Sonia. Go on Sonia.

No need to tell her. She is beautifully stubborn again and in the soul of it. Body rimed with sweat, hazel eyes straining to side step the sudden spill of the unforeseen, heart hopping with joy.

This is different, not Atlanta, not Athens. No soupy air, no seething tensions, no doubts. Dreamtime.

"I remember nothing about Atlanta," she says, "where I went, what I did, what it looked like. I'll remember everything about Sydney."

She is alone out here in Homebush. Alone with the world watching. The soft patter patter of her footsteps carrying her faster than she's ever run this distance before. She has laps and laps to go but she's happy here in the nowhere land between the leaders and the losers. She's running with her guts again.

The sound that has been in her ears all her life is there again, her own footsteps, steady and quick like a pulse. She strides out. This race won't be hers but she's back at the top of the straight, ready to give life a sprint finish again.

first published in 2000 by INPHO photographic agency, 15a lower baggot street, dublin 2, republic of ireland.

a CIP catalogue record for this book is available from the british library.

ISBN 0953430316 (hardback)

ISBN 0953430324 (softback)

photography by patrick bolger

text by tom humphries

design by cobalt

edited by patrick bolger, billy stickland and kevin gurry

origination by nicholson and bass ltd.

printed by nicholson and bass ltd.

we would like to acknowledge the generous support of the following:

Arklife

Canon

Eircell

Fuji

Image Supply Systems

Jury's Hotel Group

Kodak

The Irish Examiner

maroney, for making it all worthwhile - patrick

tom would like to dedicate this work to mary, molly and caitlin - with love

patrick would like to thank the following people for their incredible support throughout the duration of this project:

his family, friends and fellow photographers

billy stickland, tom humphries, sheena behrens, tom honan, lorraine o'sullivan, andrew paton, norman mᶜcloskey, frank malone, donal farmer, kevin gurry, elise mᶜcarthy, bernard lynch, deirdre ni chinnèide, dick bourke, bryan o'brien, ferran parades, jason clarke, brendan mᶜcarthy, denis walsh, andre gardner, tony leen, niall o'callaghan, michael maher, james meehan, robert south, mathew doyle, declan shanahan, elaine doyle, sean michael haffey, mary keane-power, stu forster, mike king, peter jess, alan storey, john and mary o'sullivan.

sonia, nick and ciara. for keeping the promise of unconditional access throughout the year. for their patience, understanding and friendship.

17.03.2000 sunset with ciara at vilamoura harbour, portugal